THRIVE
& LEAD

Strategies for Neurodivergent Employees and Their Inclusive Leaders

**JASON MICHAELS,
MBA, SPHR, SHRM-CP**

Published by Jason Michaels Publishing
Rocky Mount, Virginia, USA

ISBN: 979-8-9941876-1-6 (paperback)

First Edition: 2026
Printed in the United States of America

For permissions or inquiries, contact: info@thejasonmichaels.com
www.thejasonmichaels.com

Disclaimer

This book is intended for educational and informational purposes only. It does not provide medical, psychological, legal, or therapeutic advice, nor is it a substitute for professional diagnosis, treatment, or consultation.

The strategies, perspectives, and examples shared in this book are based on the author's personal experience and professional background in human resources. Workplace policies, legal requirements, and individual needs vary widely; readers should consult qualified professionals, including medical providers, mental health clinicians, legal counsel, or human resources experts, regarding their specific circumstances.

The author and publisher disclaim any liability arising directly or indirectly from the use of the information contained in this book.

Foreword

Reading this book was like a fireworks show in my head. Throughout the first section, sparklers went off—connecting moments I had seen or experienced throughout my career to what they truly were: different brains working in their own unique ways. It deepened my understanding of myself and sharpened my awareness of those I lead and work alongside. Whether or not someone identifies as neurodivergent, every brain operates with distinct patterns, and this book provides practical, usable tools to help leaders create environments where people can perform at their best while being fully themselves.

If the first part of the book was sparklers, the grand finale was part two, where Jason focuses on how leaders can intentionally shape workplaces that support neurodiversity. This perspective challenged me to think differently about leadership—not as a one-size-fits-all approach, but as an adaptive practice rooted in understanding how people think, process, and communicate. Jason presents these concepts in a way that is clear, relatable, and achievable, supported by actionable systems, scripts, and templates that leaders can apply immediately. This isn't about adding complexity; it's about expanding our leadership toolkit to better serve our teams.

This book strengthens leadership in three essential ways:

- How to lead more effectively

- How to support and develop others

- How to navigate and influence up the organization

For example, I have worked for an engineer for 15 years. I am not an engineer, and my brain does not work the way his does—and that difference has been one of our greatest strengths. By understanding how he processes information, what he values, and how he makes decisions, I've learned how to communicate more effectively and come prepared with the data and examples he needs. That shared understanding has created a strong, productive, and genuinely symbiotic working relationship.

I apply this same mindset to my own teams. I work intentionally to understand how each individual shows up, what clarity looks like for them, and what support enables their success. Some people need explicit direction, others need dialogue and context, and some thrive with autonomy and a clear list of deliverables. These needs evolve, because people evolve—and effective leadership recognizes and adapts to that reality.

At its core, this book is about human-centered leadership. It reminds us that success comes from recognizing individual strengths, honoring differences, and creating systems that allow people to do their best work—regardless of role or title. The skills outlined in these pages will help leaders build stronger teams, enhance communication, and cultivate workplaces where both individuals and organizations thrive.

I invite you to turn the page and explore how to amplify both your leadership impact and the potential of those around you by embracing the creativity, innovation, and strength that diversity brings to the workplace. Your brain is a gift—and this book helps you unlock its full potential.

- Megan Pittman, MAOL
Director of Administration, Bedford Regional Water Authority

Contents

Chapter 1
Start with Self-Knowledge

Understanding yourself is the foundation of everything that follows in the workplace. For neurodivergent professionals, this becomes even more essential. Self-knowledge isn't just "knowing who you are." It's understanding how you function, how your brain processes the world, what drains you, what restores you, and what conditions allow you to do your best work. It's being honest with yourself long before you try to explain anything to someone else.

I learned this earlier than most. I was diagnosed with ADD at age five, and the message was usually framed in terms of deficits — what I struggled with, what needed fixing, what made me difficult or disruptive. No one explained that my wiring wasn't wrong; it was simply different. It took years of lived experience, academic training, and a career in HR to understand that the way my mind works is not only workable but valuable.

The same is true for you.

A diagnosis is not required for self-knowledge. Many neurodivergent adults go through life without one. What matters is understanding the patterns that shape your behavior, energy, communication, and stress responses. This chapter is the foundation for everything that comes next.

Know Your Wiring

Your brain processes the world in its own distinct way. Whether you identify with ADHD, autism, dyslexia, dyspraxia, OCD, or a blend of traits, certain themes tend to show up:

- feeling overwhelmed more quickly than peers

- focusing intensely or struggling to focus depending on context

- overthinking communication or misreading cues

- relying on routines for stability

- experiencing sensory input more intensely or having difficulty filtering it

- working in bursts rather than at a steady pace

These tendencies aren't limitations. They're realities you can work with instead of fighting. Many neurodivergent employees get stuck because they assume their challenges reflect personal shortcomings rather than predictable patterns. Once you understand your wiring, you gain the ability to anticipate difficulties rather than react to them.

Understand Your Energy Cycle

Every neurodivergent person operates within an energy cycle — a pattern of:

- building energy

- spending energy

- recovering energy

And it's rarely linear.

Some tasks drain you quickly: meetings, constant transitions, complex social interactions, or rapid context switching. Other tasks restore energy: deep work, predictable routines, creative problem-solving, or quiet time. Without consciously recognizing these cycles, you're left guessing why some days feel effortless and others feel impossible.

Self-knowledge includes noticing:

- when you're at your best

- when you're approaching overload

- what drains you

- what helps you recover

This awareness allows you to create sustainable work habits rather than relying on willpower alone.

The Beliefs You Inherited (and Didn't Choose)

Many neurodivergent adults carry messages absorbed long before adulthood:

- "Try harder."

- "Pay attention."

- "Stop being dramatic."

- "Why can't you just...?"

- "Everyone else can do this."

- "You're too sensitive."

- "You're too much."

These aren't harmless remarks. They become internal scripts that shape workplace behavior for decades.

Because of them, you may mask your needs, overcommit, avoid asking questions, or push yourself past exhaustion. You learned early that your natural responses were inconvenient or unacceptable.

Self-knowledge means challenging those beliefs and replacing them with grounded truths:

- You are not lazy.

- You are not unpredictable.

- Your brain processes differently — and different is not defective.

Understanding the reason behind your reactions gives you the freedom to respond differently.

Know Your Stress Signals

Every neurodivergent person has early signs of overwhelm, even if they don't notice them in real time. Stress rarely begins with panic or shutdown; it starts with subtle cues:

- irritability

- difficulty shifting tasks

- increased sensory sensitivity

- trouble initiating work

- mental blankness

- emotional reactivity

- withdrawing from communication

These signals indicate that your cognitive load is reaching its limit.

Most workplaces reward pushing through, but self-knowledge means recognizing these signs early and adjusting before burnout sets in. You're not overreacting when you notice these signals — you're listening to your nervous system.

Know What Helps You Thrive

You need clarity, predictability, and structure. These aren't preferences; they're conditions that support strong performance.

Start identifying:

- the environments that help you focus

- the communication styles you respond to

- the levels of interaction you can manage

- the routines that improve your work

- the drains you can no longer ignore

These insights become the basis for advocating effectively — not defensively, but confidently. Later, this book will show you how to communicate these needs to your supervisor. First, you must understand them yourself.

Know Your Patterns of Masking

Masking is one of the least understood aspects of neurodivergent life. It refers to the strategies you use to appear "typical" by suppressing or altering your natural behaviors and needs.

Masking can look like:

- rehearsing what you'll say

- mimicking facial expressions or tone

- forcing eye contact

- hiding sensory discomfort

- pretending to follow when you're lost

- appearing calm while overwhelmed

Masking can be adaptive, but it is also draining. Without awareness, it becomes automatic and invisible — even to you.

Self-knowledge starts with noticing:

- when you mask

- why you mask

- what masking protects

- what it costs

This awareness helps you choose when masking is necessary and when it's harming you.

You Are Not Alone (Even If It Feels That Way)

Across industries and experience levels, neurodivergent employees tend to share one belief:

They think they are the only ones struggling in the ways they struggle.

But your patterns are shared by millions of people.

Self-knowledge helps you shift from:

"What is wrong with me?" to "My brain works differently, and I understand how to support it."

Once you see your patterns clearly, you stop fighting yourself. And when you stop fighting yourself, everything becomes more possible — emotional regulation, sustainable habits, clearer communication, and grounded self-advocacy.

This chapter is not about changing who you are. It's about finally seeing who you have always been.

Reflection Questions for Deeper Insight

Use these prompts to clarify your internal patterns:

- What aspects of my work feel intuitive and easy?

- What drains me quickly or consistently?

- What routines do I rely on?

- What do I avoid, and why?

- When do I feel most overwhelmed, and what precedes it?

- Which stress signals show up first?

- Which environments help me feel grounded and productive?

- Which environments destabilize me?

- How much of my day is spent masking?

These questions aren't for self-criticism. They're tools for understanding how you operate so you can support yourself more effectively.

Closing Insight

Self-knowledge is not optional. It is the base that supports your communication, boundaries, advocacy, leadership, and ability to thrive at work. Once you understand your wiring, you can stop blaming yourself for the challenges you face and start working with your brain instead of against it.

When you operate from that foundation, you don't just survive at work — you grow, strengthen, and begin leading yourself with clarity.

Everything else in this book builds on this beginning.

Chapter 2
Managing the Day-to-Day

Navigating daily work as a neurodivergent person isn't about pushing harder or doing more. It's about learning to work with your brain rather than forcing yourself into systems that were never designed with your wiring in mind. Day-to-day success comes from understanding your patterns, noticing what derails you. and building routines that support your energy and focus.

When you begin managing your day intentionally, the workplace becomes less overwhelming. It shifts from a series of unpredictable obstacles to something you can approach with clarity and confidence.

Build a Structure That Works for Your Mind

Most workplaces assume steady attention, predictable energy, and smooth transitions between tasks. Neurodivergent minds often work differently. You may operate in bursts need warm-up time before starting a task, or require more recovery after meetings or interruptions.

These tendencies aren't flaws — they're part of your cognitive profile. Build your daily structure around them.

Consider:

- when your focus is strongest

- which tasks feel easiest to start

- how much transition time you need

- the environment that supports your attention

- how long you can work before your mind drifts

These patterns aren't random. They're data. Once you understand the data, you can create a rhythm that aligns with how your brain naturally performs.

Start Your Day With Clarity

Beginning the day without a clear plan is one of the quickest paths to overwhelm. Neurodivergent minds often hold competing priorities in the background, and without external structure, it becomes easy to freeze, procrastinate, or jump between tasks without finishing them.

A simple morning routine can steady your entire day:

- identify your top one to three priorities

- break them into small, actionable steps

- define what "done" looks like

- group similar tasks

- note anything requiring transition time

The goal isn't perfection — it's direction. Starting your day with clarity reduces internal noise and builds momentum.

Break Tasks Into Manageable Pieces

Large or ambiguous tasks often trigger avoidance, especially when executive function is strained. Breaking work into realistic steps helps you move from "I don't know where to begin" to "I can start here."

Ask yourself:

- What is the smallest possible first step?

- What information do I need before beginning?

- What barriers make this feel bigger than it is?

Shrinking a task to a doable size removes emotional friction. Over time, breaking tasks down becomes second nature, and you become better at identifying obstacles and clarifying what you need to move forward.

Use Environmental Support Tools

Your surroundings influence how well you function. Too much stimulation can create distraction or sensory overload; too little can make it difficult to initiate or sustain focus.

Environmental support might include:
- adjusted lighting

- noise-canceling headphones

- background sound

- predictable workspace layout

- physical organizing systems

- scheduled quiet blocks

These tools aren't accommodations for weakness — they're ways to shape the environment around your strengths. The right environment doesn't change who you are; it amplifies what you do best.

Plan for Transitions, Not Just Tasks

Task transitions are one of the most underestimated challenges for neurodivergent employees. Shifting from deep concentration to a meeting or switching between different types of tasks requires real cognitive effort.

Plan for that effort.

Give yourself:
- a few minutes before meetings to shift mentally

- buffer time between tasks

- a grounding activity after intense work

- transition routines that reset your focus

These small practices reduce the "drag" that makes transitions difficult. They create the space your mind needs to move from one mode to another without losing momentum.

Use Predictability as a Strategy

Predictability lowers cognitive load. The more predictable your day is, the less energy you expend navigating uncertainty.

Look for opportunities to create consistency:

- schedule recurring tasks at set times

- group meetings together

- create predictable personal check-in routines

- establish morning and end-of-day rituals

Predictability doesn't eliminate challenges, but it stabilizes your internal system so unexpected events don't derail your entire day.

Develop Emotional Awareness Throughout the Day

Emotional intensity often fluctuates throughout the workday. Without awareness, these shifts can drive behavior in ways that feel disproportionate or confusing.

Check in with yourself:

- Am I overwhelmed?

- Am I overstimulated?

- Am I avoiding something?

- Am I running low on energy?

- Am I feeling rushed, pressured, or unclear?

These questions aren't signs that anything is wrong. They help you notice where you are so you can make adjustments before emotions escalate.

Manage Your Cognitive Load

Cognitive load is the total mental effort required to complete tasks, make decisions, process information, and navigate social expectations. Neurodivergent employees often carry higher loads because their brains filter and interpret the world differently.

Reducing load doesn't mean doing less. It means reducing friction:
- simplify communication

- break tasks into steps

- make notes for future-you instead of keeping things in your head

- automate when possible

- create systems that minimize decision fatigue

Small reductions in cognitive load accumulate into major improvements in focus, stamina, and emotional regulation.

Anticipate Overwhelm Before It Takes Over

Overwhelm builds gradually. It rarely arrives without warning — it accumulates until it becomes too heavy to push through. When you understand your early signals, you can prevent overwhelm instead of recovering from it.

Early signs may include:
- irritability

- difficulty focusing

- trouble completing tasks

- restlessness

- sensory sensitivity

- emotional shutdown

- social withdrawal

These signs are not failures. They are internal alerts. Respecting them keeps you functional and grounded throughout the day.

Build Daily Recovery Into Your Workflow

Recovery isn't something that waits until the end of the day. It should happen in short, intentional intervals during work hours.
Examples include:
- taking a brief walk

- resting your eyes

- changing environments

- spending a few minutes in quiet

- grounding or breathing exercises

- stepping away from screens

These simple resets regulate your nervous system and prevent depletion. They're not indulgent — they're essential.

Prepare for the Unexpected

Even with strong structure, surprises will happen — urgent emails, last-minute meetings, shifting priorities. Neurodivergent minds often struggle with interruptions not because of inflexibility, but because un-expected changes increase cognitive load.

Build flexibility intentionally:

- keep space open on your calendar

- add margin between major tasks

- pause and reset before responding

- re-prioritize without guilt

Flexibility isn't the opposite of structure. It's part of it. Planning for unpredictability prevents it from destabilizing your day.

Closing Insight

Managing the day-to-day isn't about perfect organization or constant productivity. It's about building a relationship with your mind that supports your strengths and doesn't punish your challenges. It's about creating habits, environments, and awareness that make success sustainable.

When you understand your patterns and work with them, you gain something much stronger than control — you gain confidence.

Confidence that you can handle what the day brings.

Confidence that you can navigate overwhelm.

Confidence that you know how to support your own success.

This is how daily management becomes daily empowerment.

Chapter 3
Navigating Communication

Effective communication is a challenge for many people, but for neuro-divergent employees, it can feel like navigating an unwritten rulebook with constantly shifting expectations. Even when your intentions are clear, the way you process information—and the way others interpret your words, tone, or timing—may not align.

These differences aren't signs of incompetence or carelessness. They reflect variations in processing, expectations, and context. Navigating communication begins with understanding how your mind works, how others communicate, and how to bridge the gap without compromising who you are.

Understanding Your Communication Style

Your communication style is shaped by:

- how quickly you process information

- how directly you speak

- how much context you need

- how overwhelmed you feel

- how you interpret tone

- how you handle ambiguity

- how you respond emotionally under stress

Neurodivergent minds often prefer clarity, precision, and honesty. Many communicate directly and value straightforward explanations. Yet workplaces frequently rely on indirect language, politeness norms, and subtle cues.

This mismatch doesn't mean you're wrong. It means your communication is optimized for a different environment.

Understanding your style helps you identify where communication challenges begin—not so you can change who you are, but so you can express yourself more effectively.

Clarity Before Expression

Many neurodivergent individuals struggle to translate internal thoughts into spoken or written communication. You may clearly understand your point but find it difficult to articulate in the moment.

Before responding, ask:

- What am I actually trying to say?

- What outcome do I want?

- What information do I need?

- What questions will help me clarify this?

Taking a moment to organize your thoughts reduces misunderstandings and helps you respond from a grounded, steady place rather than reacting under pressure.

Information Processing Differences

Neurodivergent people often process information deeply or rapidly, sometimes both. This can lead to communication patterns others misinterpret:

- needing time before responding

- answering directly when others expect nuance

- asking for additional detail

- missing implied meaning

- providing more context than expected

- using direct language perceived as blunt

- interpreting instructions literally

These behaviors reflect your processing style, not a flaw.

Simple statements like, "I process information best with clear instructions," or "I may need a moment to think before responding," prevent misunderstandings before they occur.

Managing Conversations in Real Time

In fast-paced discussions—especially meetings or group settings—communication demands increase. You may struggle to:

- track multiple topics

- interject at the right moment

- respond quickly under social pressure

- interpret tone or indirect feedback

- know when it's your turn to speak

Give yourself permission to slow the exchange when needed. Helpful supports include:

- asking clarifying questions

- writing down key points

- repeating instructions in your own words

- requesting examples

- summarizing next steps

These aren't weaknesses. They're effective communication strategies.

Email and Written Communication

Written communication can be an advantage for neurodivergent employees because it provides time to process and organize thoughts. But it also presents challenges:
- over-explaining

- long or detailed messages

- interpreting short replies as negative

- difficulty gauging urgency

- misunderstanding tone

For clearer written communication:
- keep messages focused on one topic

- use bullet points for structure

- state the purpose in the first line

- include deadlines or expectations directly

- ask whether follow-up is needed

These shifts reduce ambiguity and improve clarity for everyone involved.

Interpreting Feedback

Feedback can be emotionally complex. Neurodivergent individuals may experience it as abrupt or overwhelming, even when intended constructively. You may struggle with:

- vague or abstract feedback

- needing concrete examples

- receiving feedback publicly

- misreading tone

- emotional overload

To make feedback more manageable, ask:

- "Can you give me an example?"

- "What does success look like here?"

- "What should I focus on improving first?"

- "Can we summarize the key points?"

Clarity lowers emotional intensity and helps you understand the next steps.

Setting Communication Boundaries

Communication boundaries are essential, especially when you face interruptions, unplanned discussions, or emotionally charged interactions. Boundaries create predictability and help manage cognitive load.

Examples include:

- "Can we schedule a time to discuss this?"

- "I need a moment to process before responding."

- "I work best with clear action steps—can we outline them together?"

- "If this is urgent, please indicate it in the subject line."

Boundaries aren't barriers. They are tools that support sustainable communication.

Navigating Social Nuances

Workplace communication includes unwritten rules:
- the expected amount of small talk

- when to contribute

- when to stay quiet

- how to read group dynamics

- how to interpret indirect statements

If these nuances feel inconsistent or exhausting, you're not alone. Rather than decoding every subtle cue, focus on what you can control:
- listening carefully

- asking direct clarifying questions

- anchoring yourself in your role and responsibilities

- using predictable communication routines

- keeping interactions work-focused

You don't need to master social nuance to communicate effectively. You only need to understand what supports your success.

Handling Miscommunication

Miscommunication is inevitable, but it doesn't have to undermine your confidence.

When misunderstandings occur:

- stay curious rather than defensive

- ask what the other person heard

- restate your intention

- take responsibility without self-blame

- clarify next steps

Miscommunication doesn't mean you failed. It means two people processed the same information differently. Curiosity prevents escalation and builds trust.

When Communication Breaks Down

If communication repeatedly fails with a coworker or supervisor, self-awareness is crucial:

- Are instructions unclear?

- Are expectations shifting without notice?

- Are sensory or emotional factors affecting you?

- Are you given enough time to process?

- Is there a mismatch in communication styles?

Documenting specific patterns helps you determine the true source of the issue. This prepares you to seek support, request clarity, or adjust your approach—without assuming the problem is you.

Closing Insight

Communication is not a test you must pass. It's a skill shaped by your wiring, your environment, and the context around you. When you understand your natural communication style—and recognize that it's valid—you gain the confidence to express yourself clearly.

Navigating communication begins with understanding yourself. It grows stronger as you recognize how others communicate. And it becomes sustainable when you advocate for the conditions that help you process, respond, and connect with clarity.

You don't need to communicate like everyone else. You only need to communicate in a way that supports your success.

Chapter 4

Navigating Overwhelm and Emotional Regulation

Overwhelm shows up quickly for many neurodivergent employees. It may build quietly in the background or strike suddenly when too many demands collide. What others see as minor stressors can feel enormous when your brain processes information intensely or rapidly. Emotional regulation becomes harder, tasks feel heavier, and simple decisions can seem impossible.

Overwhelm is not a personal failure. It is a signal that your cognitive and emotional systems are overloaded. When you understand how overwhelm forms and how to regulate your response, you regain control of your workday instead of getting swept away by it.

Start by Identifying Your Overwhelm Pattern

Every neurodivergent person experiences overwhelm in a patterned way. Your triggers may differ from someone else's, but your sequence tends to be consistent. Understanding your pattern gives you a map for responding earlier and more effectively.

Ask yourself:
- What usually happens right before I shut down?

- Which situations feel the most intense?

- What emotional or physical signs appear first?

- What does my thinking feel like at each stage?

Overwhelm rarely appears without warning. Your body and mind signal the buildup long before you hit a breaking point. The sooner you recognize the pattern, the sooner you can intervene.

The Slow Build: When Overwhelm Creeps In

Sometimes overwhelm grows gradually. It may begin with irritation, trouble focusing, or small mistakes you don't typically make. You might feel tension in your body or notice your tolerance for noise, interruptions, or social interaction slipping.

Slow-build overwhelm often comes from:

- unclear expectations

- decision fatigue

- sensory overload

- too many small tasks competing for attention

- emotional residue from previous interactions

- prolonged masking

When you ignore this buildup, your system shifts from mild strain into exhaustion. Tasks that were manageable become difficult; tasks that were difficult become impossible.

Recognizing early signs lets you pause, reset, and prevent escalation.

The Sudden Spike: When Overwhelm Hits All at Once

For others, overwhelm arrives abruptly. Everything feels manageable until an unexpected change or demand pushes your system past its threshold.

Sudden overwhelm can be triggered by:
- urgent or ambiguous requests

- last-minute changes

- unexpected meetings

- emotional tone from others

- stacked interruptions

- shifts in routine

- unclear priorities

In these moments, your brain may enter "flood mode," where logical thinking becomes harder and emotional intensity surges. This is a physiological response to overload, not a character flaw.

What you need is space, clarity, and time — not pressure.

Understanding Your Emotional Regulation Bandwidth

Emotional regulation requires bandwidth — the cognitive capacity to modulate your emotional state. Neurodivergent individuals often experience fluctuating bandwidth depending on:
- sensory load

- task complexity

- social expectations

- fatigue

- earlier overwhelm

- environmental stressors

When bandwidth is low, regulating emotions becomes harder. When bandwidth is gone, it can feel impossible.

The goal isn't to eliminate emotional intensity. It's to understand your bandwidth so you can manage your responses before you reach your limit.

Emotional Spillover at Work

Emotional spillover occurs when stress from one situation carries into the next. Instead of resetting, the emotional weight travels with you, amplifying each new challenge. Because neurodivergent minds often process emotions deeply, spillover can be especially strong.
Examples include:
- feeling distant in a meeting after a stressful email

- struggling to focus because a conversation felt unclear

- interpreting neutral tones as negative

- avoiding communication out of fear of feedback

- shutting down because your system has no capacity left

Spillover isn't overreaction — it's overload. Recognizing it allows you to reset before it shapes your decisions or interactions.

Use Regulation Strategies That Match Your Nervous System

Different nervous systems respond to different strategies. What calms someone else may overstimulate you. The key is to experiment and notice what helps.
Effective regulation strategies include:
- stepping away briefly

- breathing exercises

- grounding statements

- sensory resets (noise control, lighting adjustments)

- writing thoughts down instead of holding them internally

- breaking tasks into smaller steps

- temporarily reducing inputs

- movement

- 60–90 seconds of quiet

These aren't coping mechanisms — they are physiological resets that bring your nervous system back into a state where thought and emotion reconnect.

Preventative Emotional Regulation

Regulation becomes easier when you rely on preventative habits, not just reactive strategies. Prevention keeps your nervous system stable rather than waiting until you're overwhelmed.

Preventative practices include:

- predictable routines

- planned transition time

- limiting unnecessary meetings

- organized workspace

- communication boundaries

- checklists or visual aids

- built-in recovery moments

A stable nervous system isn't a luxury. It is a tool for sustainable performance.

Know When to Communicate Your State

You don't need to disclose every detail of your emotional experience, but sharing just enough can dramatically improve workplace interactions.
   You might say:

- "I need a moment to process this."

- "Can we schedule this for later today?"

- "I want to give this my best attention — can I follow up once I've organized next steps?"

- "I'm feeling overloaded. Can we clarify priorities?"

These statements are professional and clear. They help you navigate overwhelm without masking your state or pushing yourself into shutdown.

Resetting After Overwhelm

Overwhelm doesn't end your day. You can recover.
   Your reset might include:

- a brief walk

- a change of environment

- quiet time

- sensory grounding

- hydration or food

- reorganizing your space

- rewriting a task list

- starting with a small, achievable task

The goal isn't to power through — it's to restore your nervous system so you can function again. When you reset intentionally, clarity returns, and overwhelm loses its grip.

Closing Insight

Overwhelm isn't a flaw in your design. It's a sign that your mind is processing faster, deeper, or more intensely than the environment expects. Regulation isn't about suppressing feelings; it's about understanding your capacity and responding with awareness instead of shame.

When you acknowledge your overwhelm patterns and build supportive habits, you create space for confidence, competence, and self-trust. You stop viewing yourself as fragile and begin seeing yourself as someone with a powerful, complex mind that simply needs the right support.

This chapter isn't about making you less emotional. It's about helping you stay grounded in environments that often expect more bandwidth than you can sustainably give. With self-awareness and consistent routines, regulation becomes possible — and so does long-term success.

Chapter 5
Navigating Relationships and Social Dynamics

Workplace relationships can be supportive, motivating, and rewarding — and they can also be deeply challenging, especially for neurodivergent individuals. While many people assume the hardest part of work is the tasks themselves, most stress actually comes from social dynamics. Misunderstandings, unclear expectations, inconsistent communication styles, and unspoken norms often create friction long before performance becomes an issue.

Neurodivergent employees frequently experience social interactions differently. What feels natural to others may feel confusing, draining, or unpredictable. And because relationships are rarely structured, they require continuous interpretation, which increases cognitive load. When you understand how your mind navigates social dynamics — and how others interpret your behavior — you gain confidence and stability in every interaction.

Understanding Your Relationship Patterns

Every neurodivergent person has social patterns that shape how they connect with others. These may include:
- preferring direct communication

- taking words literally

- needing time to warm up socially

- missing subtle cues

- feeling uncertain about when to speak

- withdrawing when overwhelmed

- overexplaining to avoid misunderstandings

These patterns do not reflect a lack of social intelligence. They reflect a different mode of social processing.

Knowing your patterns doesn't limit you — it gives you a roadmap for navigating relationships with more predictability and less stress.

Consistency Matters More Than Charm

In the workplace, consistency is often more important than charisma. Coworkers build trust through reliability, clarity, and predictability — not extroversion or social ease.

If you:

- communicate updates regularly

- follow through on commitments

- respond within reasonable timeframes

- maintain professionalism

- show respect and integrity

...you will build strong working relationships, even if you are quiet, literal, or socially reserved.

Many neurodivergent employees worry about not being "social enough." But your coworkers don't need you to be the loudest voice in the room — they need to know what to expect from you.

Predictability is a relationship strength.

The Energy Cost of Social Interaction

Social interactions require more energy for many neurodivergent people. This doesn't mean you dislike others; it means socializing draws from the same cognitive resources used for focus, task management, and emotional regulation.

Once you recognize the energy cost of social interaction, you can plan more intentionally:

- limit unnecessary conversations

- avoid scheduling social and intensive tasks back-to-back

- take breaks after difficult interactions

- move into deep work after recovery

- avoid chains of meetings when possible

Social energy is a real resource. Treating it as such helps you preserve it for the interactions that matter most.

Interpreting Social Cues Without Exhaustion

Many neurodivergent individuals interpret social cues through logic rather than intuition, which means nuance requires conscious processing.

Instead of trying to decode every micro-expression or ambiguous statement, focus on cues that are reliable and observable:

- tone

- word choice

- shifts in behavior

- direct statements

- explicit requests

- the structural context of the interaction

For example:
- Shorter replies may signal frustration or urgency.

- Repeated explanations often mean someone wants reassurance.

- A scheduled meeting usually indicates importance.

You don't need to catch every subtle signal. You only need to recognize the patterns that matter.

Developing Social Scripts That Work for You

Social scripts give you structured phrasing that reduces the need to improvise during conversations. They lower anxiety, reduce cognitive load, and increase clarity.

Useful scripts include:
- "Can you help me understand what you need?"

- "Before I respond, I want to make sure I understand the details."

- "What's the priority for this task?"

- "Do you have an example of what success looks like?"

- "I appreciate the feedback — what should I focus on first?"

These aren't rigid or inauthentic. They're tools that help communication feel more predictable.

Managing Workplace Friendships

Workplace friendships can be meaningful, but they can also become complicated, especially when emotional intensity, misunderstandings, or unclear boundaries appear.

Neurodivergent employees may:
- bond quickly

- overshare unintentionally

- develop strong attachments

- misinterpret friendliness as closeness

- feel confused by inconsistent behavior

- struggle when relationships shift

- feel responsible for others' emotions

Healthy workplace friendships rely on boundaries and predictability. Ask yourself:
- Does this friendship support or drain me?

- Do I understand the boundaries?

- Am I assuming closeness that hasn't been defined?

- Am I carrying emotional weight that isn't mine?

Meaningful connection at work is possible — as long as it stays balanced, respectful, and grounded.

Handling Conflict Without Emotional Overload

Conflict is difficult for many people, but it can be especially overwhelming for neurodivergent individuals. The intensity often stems from:
- fear of misunderstanding

- fear of disappointing others

- difficulty interpreting tone

- sensory overload

- unexpected changes

- emotional residue from past conflicts

To navigate conflict more effectively:
1. Slow the pace. You don't need to respond immediately.

2. Clarify the core issue. Many conflicts arise from unclear expectations.

3. Separate tone from content. Focus on the message, not the delivery.

4. Use simple clarifying statements:

   ○ "Help me understand what isn't working."

   ○ "What outcome are you looking for?"

   ○ "What needs to change moving forward?"

When conflict becomes a problem-solving conversation, it loses much of its emotional weight.

When Others Misinterpret You

Neurodivergent individuals are often misunderstood — not because they've done something wrong, but because others rely on tone reading and assumptions that don't match neurodivergent communication styles.

Common misinterpretations include:
- perceived bluntness

- seeming disinterested

- appearing overly intense

- being too quiet

- asking too many questions

- responding slowly

- looking distracted

When this happens:
- restate your intention

- clarify your meaning

- ask what the other person understood

- keep your response calm and grounded

Most misunderstandings resolve quickly once the intention is clarified.

Recognizing Social Exhaustion

Just as task overload leads to cognitive overwhelm, social overload leads to social exhaustion. Signs may include:
- irritability

- withdrawal

- difficulty focusing

- trouble finding words

- emotional numbness

- shutdown

- trouble reading cues

- avoidance

Social exhaustion isn't about disliking others. It's about needing recovery time.
Helpful resets include:

- stepping away briefly

- reducing sensory input

- hydrating or eating something grounding

- sitting somewhere calm

- listening to steady background sound

These moments help stabilize your system so you can return to interactions without burnout.

Separating Social Value From Performance Value

Many neurodivergent employees fear they're "bad at socializing," which leads them to underestimate their professional value. But performance is measured by far more than social ease:

- reliability

- quality of work

- problem-solving

- creativity

- insight

- work ethic

- follow-through

- integrity

You do not need to excel at small talk or office politics to be a strong contributor.

Your value lies in what you bring to the work — not how smoothly you navigate every social nuance.

Closing Insight

Workplace relationships are complex for everyone, but neurodivergent individuals often experience them with deeper processing, heightened intensity, and more emotional nuance. When you understand your social patterns, respect your energy limits, and communicate with clarity, you reduce anxiety and build stronger, healthier relationships.

You don't need to master every social rule to be respected. You only need to understand yourself and approach relationships with awareness and intention.

When you do, relationships stop being unpredictable challenges and become spaces where you can thrive, connect, and contribute confidently.

Chapter 6
Connecting Your World with Theirs

Workplace communication never happens in isolation. Every interaction is shaped by two internal worlds: your own and the other person's. For many neurodivergent employees, frustration comes from feeling like those worlds never quite align — your intentions don't always match how you're interpreted, and others' behaviors don't always make sense from your perspective.

This chapter focuses on understanding how your internal world connects with the worlds of the people you work with. It's about building communication bridges so your strengths can be seen clearly and your needs understood without judgment. When you recognize how your patterns interact with theirs, relationships become more predictable, less draining, and easier to navigate.

Understanding That Everyone Has a Different Processing Style

Just as your thoughts, reactions, and emotional rhythms follow patterns, so do everyone else's. People vary in:

- how quickly they process information

- how directly they communicate

- how much context they need

- how emotionally expressive they are

- how sensitive they are to tone

- how quickly they shift between tasks

- how literally or metaphorically they use language

A major source of misunderstanding is assuming someone else's brain works like yours. It doesn't. Once you recognize this, you stop personalizing differences and begin seeing them as distinct processing patterns.

This shift doesn't solve every challenge, but it reduces emotional strain. You interpret others more accurately — and yourself more compassionately.

What You Express Isn't Always What They Perceive

Many neurodivergent individuals have clear intentions internally, but once communication leaves that internal world, the message can land differently than intended.

Common disconnects include:

- directness being interpreted as anger

- silence interpreted as disinterest

- requests for clarity seen as confrontation

- questions perceived as criticism

- focused attention mistaken for rigidity

- literal interpretation mistaken for stubbornness

These interpretations reflect the other person's habits and assumptions, not your intent.

Understanding this helps you respond without self-blame and without assuming the worst about yourself or others.

Your Internal Logic Makes Sense — Even If They Don't See It

Neurodivergent employees often rely on internal logic that is consistent, structured, and deeply rooted in experience. But when those logic paths aren't verbalized, others may not understand how you reached your conclusions.

Your thinking may be:

- linear

- associative

- intuitive

- pattern-based

- detail-heavy

- big-picture first

If you communicate only the final result, people may assume you skipped steps or didn't think something through.

This isn't a flaw — it's a mismatch between internal processing and external expression.

Offering a brief explanation of your reasoning when needed helps others appreciate your insight rather than misinterpreting your intent.

When Their Emotional Expression Doesn't Match Yours

People vary widely in how they express emotion. Some show emotion openly; others show very little. Neurodivergent individuals may:

- show less expression when overwhelmed

- sound flat even when calm

- sound intense when passionate

- appear distant when focused

- appear anxious when trying to speak precisely

These expressions are often misread.

Likewise, you may misinterpret others if their emotional expression feels inconsistent or excessive. It may be unclear whether someone is upset or simply speaking passionately.

Emotional expression is a style — not a measure of truth. Understanding this reduces unnecessary tension.

Interpreting Feedback Without Losing Yourself

Feedback often triggers anxiety not because neurodivergent individuals can't handle critique, but because:

- they fear being misunderstood

- they assume the worst-case scenario

- they can't immediately gauge seriousness

- they struggle to separate tone from content

- they feel uncertain about emotional intensity

A grounded approach to feedback preserves clarity and reduces overwhelm.

Internal steps include:

1. Separate emotion from information.

2. Ask clarifying questions without apologizing.

3. Identify whether the feedback concerns the task, the process, or the communication style.

4. Distinguish actionable items from personal preference.

When you focus on meaning instead of emotion, you regain control of the conversation.

Understanding Their Need for Predictability or Flexibility

You have routines and structures that stabilize you. Others do too —
shaped by personality, culture, and experience.

Their stability needs may include
- frequent updates

- concise communication

- collaborative problem-solving

- autonomy

- emotional reassurance

- precise timelines

When your patterns align, communication feels easy. When they clash,
even small interactions can feel harder.

Recognizing others' needs doesn't require masking or changing who
you are. It simply allows you to tailor communication strategically.

Your Authenticity Matters — But So Does Strategy

Authenticity is important, especially for those who have spent years
masking to fit in. But authenticity without strategy can lead to misunderstandings.

Strategic authenticity means:
- expressing yourself honestly

- choosing clarity without overexplaining

- communicating needs without apology

- adjusting timing, tone, or level of detail — not your identity

- providing context when needed

- understanding your audience without performing

This isn't changing who you are. It's presenting who you are in a way others can understand.

That is a powerful skill — and one of the most effective tools in any relationship.

Collaboration Improves When You Understand Both Worlds

When you understand:

- your communication patterns

- their communication patterns

- the assumptions both sides bring

- sensory and emotional factors

- differences in processing speed

...you build stronger collaboration with far less emotional strain.

Collaboration doesn't require sameness. It requires enough understanding to build a stable bridge between different perspectives.

Preparing for the Leadership Perspective

Throughout this section, you've learned how your internal world shapes your workplace experience. You've gained insight into your patterns, how you process the world, and how your communication style influences your interactions.

But the people you work with — especially leaders — have patterns of their own.

To create workplaces where neurodivergent employees can thrive, both sides need understanding.

The next section of this book explores the other half of the equation: **how leaders think, what they need, and how they can support neurodivergent employees effectively.**

This isn't a shift away from your experience — it's an expansion of it. When both perspectives come together, meaningful change becomes possible.

You've learned how your internal world shapes your experience of work — your patterns, your needs, and the systems that help you thrive. But every workplace interaction involves more than your internal world alone. Leaders bring their own patterns, pressures, and assumptions into the relationship. When both sides understand each other, alignment becomes possible.

Section Two Introduction - From Self-Knowledge to Shared Leadership

Up to this point, this book has spoken directly to neurodivergent professionals — to the people who have spent years navigating workplaces that weren't designed with their minds in mind. We've explored overwhelm, masking, clarity needs, communication styles, energy rhythms, and the internal systems that allow you to show up at your best. These chapters were about **understanding yourself so you can work in alignment with who you are**, not who the workplace assumes you should be.

But thriving at work doesn't happen in isolation.

Even the most self-aware, well-structured neurodivergent employee will struggle if the environment around them is chaotic, inconsistent, or built on assumptions they cannot see. The workplace is a system — and no amount of individual effort can fully compensate for a system that works against you.

That's where this next half of the book comes in.

If the first section focused on **your internal world**, this next section focuses on **the external world you work inside** — the leaders, the structures, the expectations, and the organizational habits that shape daily reality for neurodivergent employees.

Because here's the truth:

Neurodivergent people do not become high performers solely through personal strategies.

They become high performers when their environment stops fighting them.

Leaders shape that environment more than anyone else.

The way a manager communicates, structures deadlines, responds to requests for clarity, gives feedback, handles shifting priorities, and builds team norms has a direct impact on the experience — and performance — of every neurodivergent employee they lead. Clarity, predictability, psychological safety, and thoughtful structure aren't "nice to have" leadership traits. They're performance infrastructure.

This is where the two halves of the book meet:

- **You now understand your patterns.**

- **Leaders now need to understand how to work with those patterns, not against them.**

Just as you learned to identify your overwhelm signals, your energy rhythms, your communication needs, and your structural supports, leaders must learn the complementary skills: minimizing friction, clarifying expectations, building predictable systems, and removing barriers that drain cognitive and emotional capacity.

This is not about fixing people.It's about fixing the environment so the people inside it can thrive.

The next chapters shift the point of view from the employee to the leader — but not to replace your experience. These chapters expand the conversation, showing the other half of the partnership required for lasting neuroinclusion.

Leaders will learn:

- how to communicate in ways that eliminate ambiguity,

- how to structure work so ND employees can excel,

- how to create psychological safety without lowering expectations,

- how to coach toward strengths instead of compliance,

- how clarity frameworks support high performance for everyone,

- and how predictable leadership is the backbone of sustainable inclusion.

If the earlier chapters helped you understand your world, these chapters help leaders understand the world they create around you.

Together, these perspectives complete the picture:

Neurodivergent employees thrive through alignment.

Leaders create alignment through clarity and structure.

And organizations sustain alignment through culture and systems.

Now we turn to the leaders — the people with the most influence over whether neurodivergent talent struggles, survives. or excels. This is where understanding becomes action, and where inclusion becomes performance.

Let's begin.

Chapter 7
Leading with Awareness

Leading neurodivergent employees begins with awareness — practical, grounded understanding of how people think, process, communicate, and experience work differently. Awareness isn't a soft skill; it's a leadership capability that influences performance, retention, trust, and team stability. Leaders who understand the dynamics of neurodivergence create environments where employees can perform well without masking, burning out, or shutting down.

Awareness isn't about becoming a psychologist. It's about recognizing that different brains navigate the workplace differently and adjusting your lens so you can lead more effectively. Leaders who cultivate awareness reduce friction, prevent avoidable conflict, and support clearer communication and stronger collaboration.

Awareness Begins with Curiosity, Not Conclusions

Leadership breaks down the moment assumptions replace curiosity. Quick judgments — "they're disorganized," "they're not listening," "they're resistant to feedback" — often obscure the real issue.

Before deciding what you think is happening, ask yourself:

- What else could be true?

- Is this a pattern or a moment?

- Is my interpretation based on fact or assumption?

- Do I understand their processing style?

Curiosity is an active leadership skill. It prevents misinterpretations from escalating into performance concerns and creates psychological safety — the space where employees feel comfortable sharing information that helps you lead them more effectively.

Different Brains Process Information Differently

Not every employee absorbs or responds to information the same way. Many neurodivergent employees benefit from:

- clearer expectations

- explicit instructions

- additional processing time

- written follow-up

- time to think before responding

- fewer assumptions

- alternate ways to demonstrate understanding

This is not lowering standards.It is raising clarity.

You cannot expect consistent performance from employees who are uncertain about priorities, expectations, or success criteria. Awareness ensures your message doesn't get lost in translation.

Behavior Is Communication

Leaders often respond to the behavior they observe instead of the internal experience driving it. But behavior is information. It signals needs, challenges, or processing patterns.

Examples:

- Avoiding a task may reflect overwhelm or unclear expectations.

- Direct communication may be literal, not confrontational.

- Apparent distraction may indicate sensory overload, not disengagement.

- Asking many questions may be a need for precision, not pushback.

- Hesitation may reflect missing context, not resistance.

Leaders who interpret behavior accurately make better decisions about coaching, support, and performance management.

Your Feedback Style Matters More Than You Think

Feedback is one of the most common sources of misunderstanding. Neurodivergent employees may interpret feedback more literally or more intensely because ambiguity increases cognitive load.

Effective feedback emphasizes:

- clarity over tone

- examples over generalizations

- partnership over authority

- next steps over criticism

Employees aren't "sensitive" for needing clarity — they are asking you to articulate what success looks like. When leaders offer structured, concrete feedback, employees respond with more confidence and less defensiveness.

Effective feedback isn't softer. It's clearer.

Leaders Must Recognize Cognitive Load

Cognitive load — the mental effort required to complete tasks — varies significantly. Neurodivergent employees often carry higher load because they are processing additional sensory, emotional, or contextual information.

Signs of high load include:

- slowed task initiation

- increased mistakes

- emotional shutdown

- irritability or withdrawal

- difficulty shifting tasks

- reduced communication

- visible overwhelm

These are signs of overload, not incompetence.

Leaders who recognize cognitive load adjust expectations before burnout occurs and support more sustainable performance.

Psychological Safety Is Essential, Not Optional

Neurodivergent employees do their best work when they feel safe asking questions, requesting clarity, and expressing concerns without fear of labels or judgment. Psychological safety is a performance condition.

Leaders build psychological safety by:

- encouraging questions

- avoiding punitive reactions

- clarifying instead of assuming

- maintaining calm, steady communication

- respecting differences in processing and expression

- offering structure without micromanaging

When employees don't fear misunderstanding or misinterpretation, they can focus on the work instead of masking. The result is confidence — and stronger performance.

Intentional Communication Builds Trust

Communication is more than message content. It's timing, structure, tone, and predictability. Neurodivergent employees rely on communication that is:

- consistent

- direct

- actionable

- clear in expectations

- low in ambiguity

When expectations shift without explanation or instructions are vague, trust erodes and performance drops.

Clear communication reflects leadership responsibility. Predictable communication builds trust.

Awareness Reduces Avoidable Conflict

Many performance issues stem from misunderstandings, not capability. Awareness helps leaders distinguish between:

- unwillingness and uncertainty

- resistance and overload

- defiance and misunderstanding

- disengagement and exhaustion

- disrespect and literal communication

When leaders understand what they're seeing, interventions become fair and effective. Employees feel supported rather than scrutinized, and relationships strengthen.

Awareness Is the Foundation of Leadership Effectiveness

Your ability to lead neurodivergent employees does not depend on deep expertise. It depends on how well you observe, ask questions, listen, and clarify.

Leaders who practice awareness:

- communicate more clearly

- prevent unnecessary conflict

- coach more effectively

- deliver better feedback

- retain more talent

- build stronger teams

Awareness isn't optional. It's the base that makes every other leadership skill work.

Closing Insight: This Is Where Your Leadership Playbook Begins

Your employees bring internal worlds shaped by their processing styles, communication preferences, strengths, and challenges. In Chapters 1 through 6, you explored how those patterns influence the neurodivergent experience at work.

As a leader, your role is to understand how your internal world interacts with theirs.

Awareness is the starting point.

Support, clarity, structure, and collaboration grow from here.

Chapter 8

Accommodations That Unlock Performance

Accommodations are not favors. They are performance tools. Leaders who treat adjustments as exceptions end up managing defensiveness and burnout; leaders who see them as practical supports gain better work, stronger retention, and more stable teams. This chapter gives you a simple framework for identifying what matters, having productive conversations, and implementing adjustments that reduce friction without lowering expectations.

Your goal is not to diagnose or label. Your goal is to create conditions where different brains can deliver consistent, high-quality results.

Lead With Principles, Not Opinions

When evaluating any adjustment, anchor yourself to five core principles:

1. Clarity Over Assumption

Define outcomes, success criteria, ownership, and timelines. Unspoken expectations drain time and energy.

2. Predictability Over Surprises

Ambiguity increases cognitive load. Clear rhythms and stable expectations support sustained performance.

3. Flexibility Within Standards

Hold the what; flex the how. Standards stay firm. Methods adapt.

4. Equity Over Sameness

Treat people fairly, not identically. Sameness is not fairness when brains process work differently.

5. Iteration Over Perfection

Start small, evaluate, and adjust. Effective accommodations evolve through use, not guesswork.

Separate Compliance From Performance

You do not have to be a legal expert to lead effectively. Understand the distinction:

- **Compliance lens:** Legal requirements, policy, documentation. (Partner with HR.)

- **Performance lens:** The conditions this person needs to deliver consistently. (Your domain.)

Compliance is the floor. Your performance lens is how you create an environment where employees can actually meet the standards you've set.

A Simple, Repeatable Process (The 4D Model)

Use this cadence whenever an adjustment might help — even without a formal disclosure.

1. Discover

Observe patterns. What specifically isn't working? Initiation, switching tasks, prioritizing, noise, time pressure, ambiguity?

2. Discuss

Have a calm conversation focused on success: what helps, what hinders, and what effective performance looks like. Don't ask about medical history. Stay anchored to work conditions.

3. Design

Co-create one to three adjustments tied directly to the work. Make them measurable and time-bound.

4. Document

Capture the agreement, success criteria, and a review date. Loop in HR if appropriate. Documentation prevents drift and protects both parties. Then iterate.

The Conversation (Scripts Leaders Can Use)

Openers That Reduce Pressure

- "I want to make sure our workflow supports your best performance. What conditions help you do your best work, and what tends to get in the way?"

- "Let's align on what 'good' looks like and identify what would make consistent delivery easier."

- "Would you be open to trying a few workflow changes for 30 days and reviewing impact together?"

Clarifying Questions That Produce Actionable Insight

- "When is this task easiest — time of day, format, environment?"

- "What usually triggers delays or rework?"

- "If we changed one variable next week, which would have the biggest impact?"

Closing With Shared Ownership

- "Here's what we'll try over the next two weeks. I'll own X; you'll own Y. We'll check in next Friday to review progress."

High-Leverage Adjustments (With Performance Framing)

These low-cost adjustments often produce significant improvements. Pair each with a success metric.

1. Clarity & Task Design

- **Outcome briefs:** One-page overviews for major tasks: purpose, definition of done, constraints, examples, due dates. Metric: Fewer clarification requests; improved on-time delivery.

- **Chunking work:** Break large projects into milestones with predictable check-ins. Metric: On-schedule milestones; reduced last-minute churn.

- **Model examples:** Provide a sample or template of "good."Metric: Higher first-pass quality.

2. Time & Rhythm

- **Core hours + flexible edges:** Protect dedicated hours for collaboration; allow focus time outside that block. Metric: Better meeting/focus balance; improved cycle time.

- **Meeting compression:** Use 25- or 50-minute meetings to create transition buffers. Metric: Fewer late starts; smoother transitions.

- **Deadline scaffolding:** Interim checkpoints that stabilize the final handoff. Metric: On-time completion and less rework.

3. Communication

- **Decision memos:** Recap: what was decided, why, who owns what, and deadlines. Metric: Fewer misalignments; reduced follow-up friction.

- **Channel norms:** Agree on when to use chat vs. email vs. documents. Tag urgency explicitly. Metric: More consistent responses; fewer missed actions.

- **Think time:** Share complex questions ahead of time; set a response window. Metric: Higher-quality answers; more efficient meetings.

4. Sensory & Environment

- **Noise control:** Noise-canceling headphones, quiet zones, or remote focus blocks. Metric: Improved focus; fewer errors.

- **Lighting/seat adjustments:** Avoid fluorescent lighting, offer screen filters, or relocate seating. Metric: Reduced fatigue;

greater sustained attention.

5. Workflow & Tools

- **Visual task boards:** Transparent status and next steps (Kanban or similar).Metric: Increased throughput; fewer blocked items.

- **Checklists & templates:** Standardize recurring processes .Metric: Fewer routine mistakes; faster ramp-up.

- **Automations:** Automatic transition buffers, nudges, or reminders. Metric: Smoother handoffs; fewer manual updates.

6. Social Load & Meetings

- **Agenda-first, documents pre-sent:** Give time to process before discussing. Metric: More efficient meetings; clearer decisions.

- **Designated note-taker:** Capture actions and owners live. Metric: Stronger follow-through.

- **Optional cameras / varied participation modes:** Reduce sensory load and support clarity. Metric: Broader participation; reduced meeting fatigue.

What to Avoid (Common Leadership Pitfalls)

- **Performative flexibility:** Agreeing to changes while managing as if nothing changed.

- Pathologizing differences: Treating literal communication or directness as attitude issues.

- **Endless pilots:** Testing without a review date. Commit, evaluate, adjust.

- **One-size solutions:** Copying another employee's accommodation without confirming fit.

- **Hidden standards:** Claiming output matters but rewarding style or presence instead.

Case Snapshots (Compact Examples)

Case 1: The "Late Starter" Engineer

Afternoons were high-output; mornings were low. Core hours shifted to 11–4, stand-up moved to 11:15, and deep-work time protected. Output rose 22%, bug rates dropped, collaboration unaffected.

Case 2: The "Over-Questioning" Analyst

Clarifying questions overwhelmed peers. Outcome briefs and a defined "question window" cut question volume in half and improved first-pass accuracy.

Case 3: The "Meeting-Quiet" Project Manager

Rarely spoke in meetings but produced excellent written insights. A two-hour post-meeting written-response window improved decision quality and reduced missed timelines.

Measure What Matters

Track a few metrics for 30–60 days:
- on-time delivery

- first-pass quality

- rework hours

- clarification requests

- meeting vs. focus time

- blocked-task count

- self-reported overwhelm

- team stability signals

You're looking for directional improvement, not perfection. If results improve, keep the adjustment. If not, iterate.

When Disclosure Enters the Conversation

If an employee discloses a diagnosis or requests formal accommodations:
- Thank them — disclosure reflects trust.

- Shift into the 4D process and involve HR for documentation.

- Keep the discussion anchored to work conditions, not medical detail.

- Avoid amateur diagnostics; your role is environment, not labels.

Many effective adjustments occur without formal disclosure. The threshold for trying a workflow change is far lower than the threshold for medical documentation.

Coaching Without Coddling

Support and standards are not opposites. Effective leadership sounds like:
- "The outcome and deadline remain the same. Let's adjust the workflow so you can hit them consistently."

- "If we try these changes for two weeks, what outcome should we expect?"

- "We'll meet Fridays to review progress. If something isn't helping, we'll adjust."

Hold the bar. Change the path. That's what equity looks like in day-to-day leadership.

One-Page Accommodation Plan (Template Language)

Purpose: Improve first-pass quality and on-time delivery for [role/task].
  Adjustments (30-day pilot):
    1. Outcome briefs for major tasks (owner: leader).

    2. 25-/50-minute meetings + 10-minute transition buffers (owner: leader + team).

    3. Written decision recaps within 24 hours (owner: meeting lead).

    4. Two weekly deep-work blocks of 90 minutes each (owner: employee).

Success Criteria:
- On-time rate ≥ 90%

- Rework hours ↓ 30%

- Clarification requests ↓ 40%

Check-ins: Weekly, 15 minutes.
Review Date: [Date] — keep / modify / retire.
Keep it simple and visible.
For a full printable version of this plan, see Appendix C: One-Page Accommodation Plan.

Closing Insight

Accommodations are part of leadership craft. When you align work conditions with how people actually think and operate, performance stabilizes, relationships ease, and the team spends more time on meaningful work and less time fighting friction.

You don't have to solve everything in one conversation. Start with one adjustment that makes the work easier to do well, measure it, and iterate.

The next chapter strengthens the skills that sustain accommodations long-term: delivering clear feedback and coaching for consistency — without lowering expectations or burning out your team.

Chapter 9
Coaching That Builds Consistency

Great leadership isn't about spotting gaps; it's about closing them without eroding trust. For neurodivergent team members, the difference between "I can't" and "I can, consistently" is often a leader who coaches with clarity, predictability, and respect for how different brains learn. Coaching is not a performance workaround or a rescue mission. It's a system for helping capable people produce reliable results under conditions that fit how they process, focus, and recover.

This chapter gives you a practical way to coach neurodivergent talent so standards remain high, expectations are explicit, and growth is sustainable.

Build your coaching stance: standards + support

Coaching fails when it confuses kindness with vagueness. Your stance should be:

- **High bar, clearly defined.** Outcomes, timelines, ownership, and "definition of done" live in writing.

- **Right-sized support.** You flex the how (process, rhythm, environment), not the what (results).

- **Iterative and observable.** Small experiments, measured weekly.

- **Respectful of bandwidth.** You assume cognitive load is real and design around it.

- **Future-focused.** You coach to what success looks like next week, not to what went wrong last week.

This stance treats coaching as a performance enablement tool, not a personality makeover.

Start with precision: what problem are we actually solving?

Leaders often label issues as "communication," "motivation," or "attention," which are too broad to fix. Name the specific, observable pattern:

- **Initiation:** work starts late or stalls at first step.

- **Switching:** transitions between tasks derail momentum.

- **Prioritization:** wrong item chosen when priorities shift.

- **Detail depth:** too shallow or too deep for the context.

- **Clarification load:** too many/few questions at the wrong time.

- **Meeting strain:** live processing limits contribution.

- **Follow-through:** handoffs or closes are inconsistent.

If you can't describe the pattern in one sentence that a third party could see, you don't have a coachable target yet.

The 3C framework for feedback that lands

Neurodivergent employees often carry more cognitive and emotional load during feedback. Reduce ambiguity with **Context → Conduct → Change:**

1. **Context** — anchor to work outcomes "For the quarterly dashboard project due Friday..."

2. **Conduct** — describe what was observed (no mind-reading) "...the

first draft arrived without the variance notes we agreed on."

3. **Change** — specify the next-time behavior and support

"Next time, include the three variance notes in the draft checklist. I'll attach the template so it's easy to tick off."
Close with a check for clarity, not agreement:
"What will you do differently on Wednesday's draft, and what—if anything—do you need from me?"
Short, concrete, respectful. No sermons, no speculation.

CLEAR Coaching Model (Neuroinclusive Version)

Why keep CLEAR? It gives leaders a predictable route through any coaching conversation while leaving room for individual processing needs. Use CLEAR for the conversation arc; use **3C** for concise feedback and **4R** for weekly cadence.

C — Contract (Agree the goal & guardrails)

Purpose: Name the target, scope, timeline, and roles so the conversation has borders and the employee has safety.
Leader prompts
- "What outcome would be most useful to focus on today?"

- "By the end of this conversation, what would you like to leave with?"

- "We'll stay on this topic for 15 minutes and end with a next step—sound good?"

Neuroinclusive notes
- Offer an agenda or questions in advance when possible.

- State time limits and what 'done" looks like for the meeting.

L — Listen (Surface the reality without judgment)

Purpose: Understand the employee's experience, not just the symptoms you've observed.

Leader prompts
- "Walk me through what happens from 'task assigned' to 'task delivered.'"

- "Where does friction show up first—starting, switching, or finishing?"

- "What conditions were present the last time this went well?"

Neuroinclusive notes
- Allow silence and thinking time.

- Reflect back facts you heard; avoid interpreting tone.

E — Explore (Co-diagnose levers, not the person)

Purpose: Identify a small number of high-leverage adjustments (clarity, rhythm, workflow, communication, environment).

Leader prompts
- "If we changed one variable next week, which would help most?"

- "Would chunking the work, a mid-point check, or a written brief reduce rework?"

- "Where do you want more autonomy, and where would structure help?"

Neuroinclusive notes
- Focus on work conditions, not traits.

- Tie each idea to a simple metric (on-time, first-pass quality, rework hours).

A — Action (Commit to one change with an owner and metric)

Purpose: Turn insight into a tiny experiment with a clear success signal.
Leader script
- "For two weeks, we'll try: • Outcome brief for major tasks (I own) • 10 a.m. outline checkpoint (you own) • Decision recap within 24 hours (meeting lead owns) Success looks like on-time ≥ 90% and rework ↓ 30%. We'll review Fridays."

Neuroinclusive notes
- Favor one or two actions only. Over-stuffing kills follow-through.

- Write it down. Predictability lowers load.

R — Review (Close the loop & iterate)

Purpose: Check the experiment against the metric, keep what works, swap what doesn't.
Leader prompts
- "What improved? What didn't? What do we keep, change, or drop?"

- "Do we need a different lever—clarity, rhythm, workflow, communication, or environment?"

Neuroinclusive notes
- Keep the review cadence steady (see 4R). Consistency builds trust and momentum.

How CLEAR fits with the rest of Chapter 9

- **3C (Context → Conduct → Change)** gives you crisp feedback lines inside the conversation.

- **CLEAR** provides the *conversation arc*.

- **4R (Recap → Results → Refine → Reset)** is your *weekly coaching cadence* that sustains the change.

Think: **3C = sentences, CLEAR = session, 4R = cycle**.

Example (90-second CLEAR in practice)

- **Contract:** "Let's focus on the monthly report misses. In 15 minutes, we'll leave with one change to test."

- **Listen:** Employee shares they start late because the brief is fuzzy and meetings stack around the draft time.

- **Explore:** You discuss two levers: a one-pager brief and a 10 a.m. outline checkpoint.

- **Action:** "For two weeks: I'll provide an outcome brief; you'll post the outline by 10 a.m. We'll measure on-time and rework."

- **Review:** Friday 15-minute check; keep if metrics improve.

- **Full template: see Appendix B — Leader Tools, Template B1 (CLEAR Coaching One-Pager).**

Pitfalls (and fixes)

- **Vague Contract:** The talk meanders. → *Write the goal in one line at the top.*

- **Listening for rebuttal:** You plan your reply. → *Reflect back facts first; then explore.*

- **Too many actions:** Nothing sticks. → *One change, two max, two weeks.*

- **No Review date:** Drift returns. → *Put the review on the calendar now.*

Coach with the 4R cadence (15 minutes, weekly)

High-functioning coaching is light, frequent, and predictable. Use this weekly structure:

1. **Recap** (2 min) — "What did we commit to last week?"

2. **Results** (6 min) — "What worked, what didn't, what changed?" (glance at metrics)

3. **Refine** (5 min) — adjust 1–2 levers (process, clarity, environment)

4. **Reset** (2 min) — confirm next steps, owners, dates

Put it on the calendar at the same time every week. Predictability lowers load and builds momentum.

Levers that reliably improve consistency

Tie each lever to a metric so you can tell if coaching works.

1) Clarity

- One-page outcome briefs; checklist at "definition of done."

- *Metric:* first-pass quality; rework hours.

2) Rhythm

- Core collaboration hours + protected deep-work blocks; 25/50-minute meetings with transition buffers.

- *Metric:* on-time delivery; context-switch fatigue reports.

3) Workflow

- Visual board (To Do / Doing / Done) with owner next step; interim milestones.

- *Metric*: blocked items; cycle time.

4) Communication

- Decision recaps within 24 hours; question windows after assignment; channel norms.

- *Metric*: clarification pings; misalignment incidents.

5) Environment

- Noise/lighting adjustments; camera-optional meetings; pre-reads for complex topics.

- *Metric*: meeting contribution; error rate in deep work.

Change one lever at a time. Observe. Iterate.

What to say in the moment (leader scripts)

When initiation stalls

"Let's shrink the first step: by 11 a.m., post the outline. I'll react, then you build section one. We'll checkpoint at 3 p.m."

When detail depth is off

"For this audience, two bullets per insight is 'enough.' If you have more, put them in an appendix."

When meetings drain contribution

"Read the doc beforehand and post comments by noon. In the meeting, you can add via chat. We'll capture decisions live."

When priorities shift

"Today, A over B. If that changes, I'll message 'PRIORITY SWAP' so you don't guess."

When emotions spike

"Let's pause and write the steps. We'll reconvene in 10. I want the plan, not a perfect reaction."

Direct, calm, specific—without pathologizing the person.

Coach the skill, not the style

Avoid grading "professionalism" as a vibe. Coach **skills you can see:**

- breaking work into steps

- sequencing and time-boxing

- drafting before polishing

- summarizing decisions

- escalating blocks early

- closing the loop on handoffs

If it can't be observed and measured, it's not a coaching target.

Document lightly so progress sticks

Two simple artifacts keep coaching from becoming opinion vs. opinion:

- **Coaching Notes (shared doc):** date, target, lever, metric, next step.

- **Decision Log (team-visible):** what/why/owner/when.

These reduce memory load, align expectations, and de-risk handoffs.

Strengths-based coaching (without turning into flattery)

"Strengths-based" doesn't mean ignoring gaps. It means **placing the work where strengths carry the weight:**

- leverage hyperfocus for deep analysis, not live debate

- channel pattern recognition into risk spotting or QA

- use literal communication for crisp documentation

- assign facilitation to a teammate; assign synthesis to the ND employee

Don't try to make everyone good at everything. Make the team great by design.

When performance truly dips: the two-track approach

If results slip despite coaching, separate **enablement** from **accountability**:

- **Enablement track:** keep the 4R cadence and levers focused on improvement.

- **Accountability track:** set explicit performance expectations with time-bound goals, written support, and clear consequences if unmet.

Tell the truth kindly:
"Here's the standard. Here's the support. Here's the timeline. We'll review on [date]."
This is fair to the employee and to the team.

Pitfalls to avoid (they look small; they cost you big)

- **Vague praise, sharp critiques**. Balance both with specifics.

- **Moving targets.** Change priorities, but label the change loudly.

- **Coaching by autobiography.** What works for you may not fit their brain.

- **Over-indexing on meetings.** Written thinking often outperforms live processing.

- **No end to experiments.** Every adjustment needs a review date.

Case snapshots

Case 1 — The analyst who "sat on" work

Work started late; deliverables compressed into the final day. The leader added a 10 a.m. outline checkpoint and a 3 p.m. first-draft checkpoint, plus 25-minute meetings. On-time delivery rose from 60% to 92% in four weeks.

Case 2 — The PM who "vanished" after meetings

Live processing depleted her; follow-through lagged. The leader moved decisions into a doc with 24-hour recap and assigned action owners in the meeting. Follow-through consistency climbed; team escalations dropped by half.

Case 3 — The engineer labeled "overly blunt"

Literal updates triggered friction. The leader set a written update template: status, blocker, next step. ask. Conflicts cooled; velocity improved.

Light metrics that tell you coaching is working

Track two or three for 30–45 days:
- first-pass quality

- on-time delivery

- rework hours

- blocked-item count

- clarification pings per task

- self-reported overwhelm (1–5)

- meeting-to-focus ratio

If the line trends in the right direction, keep the lever. If not, swap the lever—don't raise your voice.

Closing insight

Coaching isn't extra work; it's how the work gets predictable. When you coach with clarity, cadence, and respect for bandwidth, neurodivergent employees don't just cope—they compound their strengths. You get fewer surprises, steadier delivery, and a team that trusts your process because it works.

In the next chapter, we'll build on this by tightening **performance clarity and decision frameworks**—so expectations are explicit, trade-offs are faster, and your team knows exactly how to succeed.

Chapter 10

Building Neuroinclusive Teams & Cultures

A neuroinclusive culture is not created through slogans, training sessions, or well-intentioned posters about inclusion. It is created through predictable behaviors, clear systems, explicit norms, and leadership habits that support different cognitive styles. When leaders understand how culture shapes the daily reality of neurodivergent employees, they stop treating inclusion as a side initiative and start treating it as part of operational excellence.

Culture is the environment people work inside. It determines whether neurodivergent employees can participate fully, communicate comfortably, and contribute consistently. This chapter outlines how leaders build teams where differences are understood, supported, and leveraged—where structure reduces cognitive friction, communication is predictable, and trust becomes part of the workflow.

Culture Is Built from What Leaders Tolerate and What They Repeat

Culture forms through two forces:

1. **What leaders reinforce** Clarity, communication norms, psychological safety, stable systems, and predictable decisions.

2. **What leaders allow** Ambiguity, hidden rules, inconsistent feedback, unspoken expectations, and interpersonal friction.

Neurodivergent employees feel the impact of culture more intensely than others.

Where ambiguity exists, cognitive load increases.

Where predictability exists, performance stabilizes.

Leaders set the tone—not by announcing values, but by choosing what becomes standard and what does not.

Psychological Safety: The Foundation of Neuroinclusive Teams

Psychological safety isn't about making everyone comfortable. It's about making it safe to participate without penalty. For neurodivergent employees, psychological safety means they can:

- Ask clarifying questions

- Request structure or predictability

- Express confusion without embarrassment

- Communicate differently

- Share challenges early

- Admit when a workflow doesn't align with their processing style

Safety is created by *behavior*, not intention.

Leaders reinforce psychological safety when they:

- Respond to questions with patience, not irritation

- Provide clarity rather than criticism

- Offer multiple ways to contribute (verbal, written, asynchronous)

- Acknowledge differences in processing and communication

- Name expectation shifts explicitly

When these behaviors are predictable, team members stop burning energy on self-protection and redirect it into the work.

Team Norms That Reduce Cognitive Load

Culture becomes real when expectations are written, shared, and stable. Neurodivergent employees thrive in environments where norms are explicit.

Consider establishing norms such as:

- **Clarity First:** Define outcomes, ownership, timelines, and success criteria.

- **Visible Priorities:** Label priority changes ("PRIORITY SWAP"), don't imply them.

- **Predictable Communication:** Set channel norms (chat for quick updates, email for decisions, docs for collaboration).

- **Process Transparency:** Write down decisions, rationale, and next steps.

- **Respect for Processing Styles:** Thinking time is normal; instant responses are optional.

- **Meetings with Modes:** Permit live, written, or post-meeting participation.

These norms stabilize the environment and support neurodivergent minds by reducing guesswork and preventing invisible performance traps.

How Clarity Supports Culture (Without Overrunning the Chapter)

Clarity frameworks like the Outcome Brief, FAST decision model, and RAID ownership structure strengthen culture by removing ambiguity. They work best when positioned as cultural tools, not bureaucratic hoops.

Clarity tools:
- Stabilize expectations

- Reduce rework

- Lower anxiety

- Support autonomy

- Provide predictable structures

- Make decision pathways transparent

Where clarity meets inclusion:
- **Outcome Briefs** give neurodivergent employees a stable reference point.

- **RAID** reduces confusion about decision authority.

- **FAST** removes opaque decision-making that leaves employees guessing.

These tools are not the culture—they are the scaffolding that makes the culture functional and equitable.

Reducing Hidden Rules: The Silent Threat to Neurodivergent Employees

Hidden rules create inequity because they are invisible, unspoken, and often arbitrary. Examples include:
- "Speak up quickly or you'll lose your chance."

- "If you need help, hint at it indirectly."

- "Real decisions happen in meetings."

- "Interrupting shows engagement."

Neurodivergent employees often fail tests they never knew existed.

Leaders eliminate hidden rules by:

- Naming expectations aloud

- Discussing unwritten norms, then rewriting them

- Explaining how decisions are truly made

- Normalizing multiple communication styles

- Clarifying what certain behaviors do and do not signal

When everything is explicit, everyone stops guessing and starts performing.

Communication Systems That Work for All Brains

Teams often assume communication is simply "how we talk." But neuroinclusive communication requires predictable rhythms and multiple modes.

Multiple Participation Modes

- Verbal

- Written

- Asynchronous

- Structured forms

Predictable Rhythms

- Weekly check-ins

- Standing agendas

- Pre-distributed materials

- Decision recaps

Low-Interpretation Communication

- Clear subject lines

- Explicit deadlines

- Labeled priorities

- Concise action items

These systems reduce cognitive friction and make the team easier to navigate—for everyone.

Designing Meetings for Neurodivergent Minds

Meetings often reward fast processors, extroverts, and people skilled at in-the-moment synthesis. Neuroinclusive meetings level the field by:
- Sending agendas and materials in advance

- Allowing written input before and after

- Assigning roles (facilitator, note-taker, decision owner)

- Separating debate from decision

- Reducing sensory strain (camera-optional, quieter environments, structured flow)

When meetings aren't endurance tests, participation improves—and so does the quality of decisions.

Team Rituals That Reinforce Inclusion

Culture isn't built in annual events; it's built in daily repetition.
Effective rituals include:

- **Weekly Clarity Reset:** Align on priorities, expectations, and obstacles.

- **Wins & Workflows:** Celebrate strengths and examine processes, not personalities.

- **Decision Review Fridays:** Publish decisions and owners in a visible log.

- **Workstyle Spotlights:** Quick shares about each person's optimal work patterns.

Rituals make inclusion predictable. Repetition makes inclusion cultural.

Culture Is Maintained Through Systems, Not Enthusiasm

Enthusiasm fades. Systems persist.

Neurodivergent employees need consistency more than inspiration. Sustainable cultures rely on:

- Written norms

- Shared tools

- Defined processes

- Decision visibility

- Clear roles and ownership

- Lightweight metrics

- Leadership stability

When these elements are embedded, culture survives turnover, reorgs, and busy seasons.

Case Snapshots

Case 1 — The Team That Removed Hidden Rules

A marketing team mapped unwritten norms and replaced them with explicit expectations. The ND coordinator reported "less guessing, more doing," and on-time delivery improved substantially.

Case 2 — The Designer Who Didn't Speak in Meetings

The leader introduced asynchronous input and a shared meeting notes document. The designer became the team's strongest synthesizer and most reliable decision clarifier.

Case 3 — The Analyst Overwhelmed by Shifting Priorities

A Priority Board labeled HOT / SWAP / HOLD reduced cognitive overload and stabilized execution.

Closing Insight

Culture is not what leaders *say*—it is what they *systemize*. Neuroinclusive cultures thrive when leaders create:

- Clarity

- Predictability

- Explicit expectations

- Multiple communication paths

- Transparent decisions

- Stable norms

When these elements are present, neurodivergent employees don't just fit in—they elevate the team.

The next chapter will connect culture to sustainability: how to keep these practices alive over time and through organizational change.

Chapter 11
Building Sustainably: Keeping Neuroinclusion Alive

Neuroinclusion isn't achieved through goodwill, awareness campaigns, or inspirational posters in break rooms. It's achieved through systems, habits, and leadership practices that hold up even when the pressure is on. If the earlier chapters of this book focused on understanding yourself, clarifying expectations, and building aligned working relationships, this chapter focuses on long-term sustainability — the part organizations often overlook.

Because here is the truth no one likes to say out loud:

Neuroinclusion dies fastest when it depends on individual effort alone.

A neurodivergent employee can do everything right — communicate clearly, manage their energy, structure their workday, advocate for their needs — and still burn out if the organization around them doesn't reinforce that effort.

Likewise, a leader can implement every clarity tool, coach well, build predictable routines, and still fail to sustain inclusion if the culture doesn't support them, if upper leadership contradicts their work, or if the environment rewards fire drills over foresight.

Sustainability means moving from:

individual effort → system-driven success.

And that shift is what carries neuroinclusion into the future.

The Hidden Threat to Neuroinclusion: Reversion Pressure

Every workplace has gravity.

Without ongoing structure, systems decay.

Without reinforcement, habits slip.

Without clarity, teams drift back into chaos.

Reversion pressure happens when:

- A deadline is tight

- A priority shifts suddenly

- A reorganization hits

- A new manager arrives

- Stress skyrockets

- The company changes strategy

- Turnover shakes a team

- Someone "just needs something fast"

In those moments, workplaces often default to:

- vague expectations

- unstated assumptions

- rapid-fire communication

- constant context switching

- informal decision-making

- "figure it out" mentalities

- masking as a survival tactic

- performance over well-being

For neurodivergent employees, this shift is not merely inconvenient — it is destabilizing.For leaders, it can feel like losing control of a system they were trying to build.

Sustainable neuroinclusion requires anticipating reversion pressure and designing ways to withstand it.

Sustainability Principle #1: Clarity Must Become Cultural, Not Situational

If clarity only happens when a leader "has time," it fails.If predictability only happens when everything is calm, it fails.If accommodations only work when workloads are light, they fail.

Clarity must become **how the team works**, not **what the leader does when things are ideal.**

Here's what cultural clarity looks like:

- Expectations are documented, not implied.

- Workflows are predictable even when priorities shift.

- Decisions are summarized the same way every time.

- Changes are communicated consistently across managers.

- Accommodation processes are standardized.

- Everyone knows where information lives.

- Leaders ask clarifying questions before giving direction.

- Teams default to structure, not improvisation.

Clarity becomes a habit, not a heroic effort.

Sustainability Principle #2: Systems Must Outlive the People Who Built Them

This is where most organizations fail.

A manager who champions neuroinclusion leaves.A new VP arrives with a different leadership style.The culture tilts toward urgency, speed, and "just make it happen."And suddenly, the environment neurodivergent employees thrived in begins collapsing.

Sustainable systems are built to withstand personnel changes:

- Documentation survives leadership turnover.

- Team norms survive reorganizations.

- Meeting structures survive role transitions.

- Accommodation plans survive manager changes.

- Clarity frameworks survive shifting priorities.

If your neuroinclusion strategy depends on a single leader, it is not a strategy — it is a personality trait.

A sustainable system is one where:

your practices survive your absence.

Sustainability Principle #3: Feedback Loops Keep Inclusion Healthy

Workplaces drift.People drift.Processes drift.

Feedback loops—simple, predictable mechanisms—pull teams back into alignment.

Examples:

Monthly clarity audits

Teams review:

- What's working

- What's unclear

- What's drifting

- What needs redefining

Quarterly accommodation reviews

Employees confirm whether their needs are being met or need updating.

Team norm refreshers

Revisit agreements, revise them, recommit to them.

Leader self-checks

Leaders ask:
- Am I assuming understanding?

- Am I updating expectations clearly?

- Am I overloading people without noticing?

- Am I modeling the behaviors I expect?

Feedback loops are maintenance for the system — the organizational equivalent of brushing your teeth.

Sustainability Principle #4: Neurodivergent Employees Need Predictable Safe Channels

One of the biggest sources of ND burnout is not the work itself, but the **uncertainty about where to take concerns.**

A sustainable environment guarantees:
- A predictable feedback channel

- Multiple avenues for clarification

- A clear escalation path that doesn't feel punitive

- A way to revisit expectations without embarrassment

- Spaces where stating limitations is normalized

- Psychological safety that doesn't vanish when stress rises

When safe channels are predictable, ND employees spend less time masking and more time doing meaningful work.

Sustainability Principle #5: Leadership Alignment Must Be Proactive

A single inclusive manager cannot compensate for misaligned senior leadership.

To sustain neuroinclusion long-term:

- Senior leaders must support predictability.

- HR must reinforce clear processes.

- Teams must share norms, not develop them ad hoc.

- Written expectations must be standardized across managers.

- Onboarding must set clarity expectations from day one.

When leaders at every level operate from the same playbook, ND employees experience stability instead of mixed signals.

How the Two Halves of This Book Come Together

The first half of this book helped neurodivergent professionals:

- understand their patterns

- clarify their needs

- structure their work

- communicate more effectively

- identify overwhelm before it spirals

- create internal systems to thrive

The second half helped leaders:
- remove organizational friction

- provide clarity

- build predictable environments

- give effective feedback

- design workflows that reduce cognitive load

- coach with respect and precision

- build inclusive cultures

Together, these halves form a powerful reality:

Neuroinclusion is not solely the employee's responsibility.

Neuroinclusion is not solely the leader's responsibility.
Neuroinclusion is a shared system — built, maintained, and strengthened from both directions.**
Both sides require clarity.
Both sides require communication.
Both sides require understanding.
Both sides require structure.
Both sides require humanity.
This is the relationship that sustains neurodivergent talent — and unlocks exceptional performance.

The Future of Neuroinclusion

The workplace is changing.

Neurodivergent employees are no longer invisible, silent, or forced to mask to survive.

Leaders are learning that inclusion is not an accommodation request form — it is a culture built through consistent behaviors.

Organizations are beginning to understand that clarity helps everyone, not just those who struggle without it.

But progress is not guaranteed.

Neuroinclusion will flourish only if organizations:

- build durable systems,

- maintain predictable practices,

- protect psychological safety under pressure,

- and treat structure as a core leadership behavior, not an optional trait.

The opportunity ahead is enormous.

A Final Message to Neurodivergent Professionals

You are not defective.

You are not difficult.

You are not "too much."

You are not a problem to fix.

You are someone whose mind works differently — and differently is valuable.

Your brilliance does not come from masking. It does not come from contorting yourself into neurotypical expectations.

It comes from your strengths, your insight, your honesty, your creativity, your resilience, your unique rhythm, and the way you see patterns others miss.

Thriving is not a fantasy.

It is a structure.

A partnership.

A system.

A set of choices — by you and by your leaders.

A Final Message to Leaders

You have the power to create environments where neurodivergent employees truly shine.
Not by fixing them.
Not by coaching them into conformity.
Not by softening expectations.
By providing:

- clarity

- predictability

- meaningful feedback

- thoughtful structure

- psychological safety

- and a culture where diversity of thought is an asset, not an obstacle

You are not just leading employees — you are shaping the conditions where excellence becomes possible.
Your clarity can transform someone's entire career.
Your predictability can reduce years of stress.
Your support can unlock exceptional performance.
You can be the leader someone always hoped to have.

Closing Thought

The workplace grows stronger when people stop wasting energy pretending and start using that energy contributing.
Neuroinclusion is not a trend.It is not a special program.It is not a temporary initiative.
It is the future of work.

And with the right systems, the right leaders, and the right understanding, it is a future where neurodivergent people can not only survive — **but thrive and lead**.

References

Neurodiversity & Cognitive Variation

Baker, K. *Neurodiversity and the Workplace.*
Grandin, T. *Thinking in Pictures.*
Kaufman, S. B. *Ungifted: Intelligence Redefined.*
Pollak, D. (Ed.). *Neurodiversity in Higher Education.*
Singer, J. *NeuroDiversity: The Birth of an Idea.*
Walker, N. *Neuroqueer Heresies.*

Neurodivergent Identity, Processing & Psychology

Gordon, D. *The Autistic Mind Finally Speaks.*
Hallowell, E. M., & Ratey, J. J. *Driven to Distraction (Revised and Updated).*
Price, D. *Unmasking Autism.*
Treffert, D. *Islands of Genius.*
Walker, N., & Raymaker, D. *Autistic Academic.*

Workplace Inclusion, Leadership & Organizational Design

Austin, R., & Pisano, G. "Neurodiversity as a Competitive Advantage." *Harvard Business Review.*
Cooper, D., & Radcliffe, N. *The Neurodivergent Workplace.*
Friedman, S. D., & Westring, A. F. *Total Leadership.*
Hobbs, R. *The Neurodivergent Professional.*
Maguire, K. *Workplace Neurodiversity Rising.*

McKinsey & Company. *Research on psychological safety and cognitive diversity.*

Newman, B. *The Hidden Curriculum of Work.*

Communication, Coaching & Behavior Change

Brown, B. *Dare to Lead.*

Edmondson, A. *The Fearless Organization.*

Goldsmith, M. *What Got You Here Won't Get You There.*

Heath, C., & Heath, D. *Switch.*

Rock, D., & Cox, C. "SCARF Model." *NeuroLeadership Institute Journal.*

Stone, D., Heen, S., & Patton, B. *Difficult Conversations.*

Emotional Regulation, Cognitive Load & Human Behavior

Baumeister, R. F. *Willpower.*

Kahneman, D. *Thinking, Fast and Slow.*

Sapolsky, R. *Behave.*

Siegel, D. J. *The Developing Mind.*

Legal & Compliance Foundations

ADA National Network. Employer guidance and fact sheets.

Equal Employment Opportunity Commission. Guidance on reasonable accommodation.

SHRM. ADA and workplace inclusion resources.

HRCI. Accommodation and compliance best practices.

Sources Connected to the Book's Tools & Frameworks

Edmondson — psychological safety research.

Rock & Cox — SCARF model for interpreting behavior.

Hallowell & Ratey — executive function and overwhelm.

Price, Pollak, Walker — masking, social load, communication differences.

Neurodiversity in Business Consortium — workplace standards.

Austin & Pisano — business case for neurodiversity.

Stanford Neurodiversity Project — environmental and systems-level design.

Appendix A: Neurodivergent Self-Tools (Employee Playbook)

These tools support the first half of your book, giving neurodivergent employees practical ways to understand themselves, plan their work, and communicate their needs clearly.

A1. Self-Knowledge Worksheet

Purpose: Identify how your brain works so you can advocate effectively.

1. My Strength Patterns
List 5 activities where you consistently excel:

-
-
-
-
-

2. My Activation Triggers
What helps you start tasks? (Examples: deadlines, body doubling, timers, visuals)

-

-

-

3. My Processing Style
Check all that apply:
☐ Verbal processor
☐ Written/visual processor
☐ Needs time to think
☐ Detail-first
☐ Big-picture-first
4. My Cognitive Load Signals
How can I tell I'm overwhelmed?
5. Ideal Work Conditions
Environment, communication preferences, timing, structure:

A2. Strengths Mapping Template

Use this to match your strengths with tasks and environments.

Strength	How I Use It	Tasks That Fit	Tasks That Drain Me

A3. Focus & Rhythm Planning Sheet

Weekly Setup:
- **Focus Blocks:**

When I do my best deep work → _____
- **Recovery Patterns:**

What resets me? _____
- **Transition Needs:**

How I switch tasks effectively _____

Daily Rhythm:
Time of Day Best for Notes:
Morning
Midday
Afternoon
Late Day

A4. Communication Preference Overview

Complete and share with your leader if desired.
I communicate best when:
I prefer to receive instructions:
☐ Verbally with recap
☐ Written (ideal)
☐ With examples
☐ With definitions of done
☐ With milestones
Follow-up questions:
☐ As needed
☐ Scheduled
☐ Written preferred

A5. Sensory Inventory Checklist

Check what affects your focus:
Environment
☐ Noise
☐ Lighting
☐ Temperature
☐ Visual clutter

☐ Strong smells

Tools that help

☐ Noise-canceling headphones

☐ Alternate seating

☐ Camera-optional meetings

☐ Written materials

☐ Break spaces

Write any additional needs:

Appendix B: Leader Tools & Templates

These tools support Chapters 7–11 and reflect the clarity, coaching, and culture frameworks leaders rely on.

B1. CLEAR Coaching Template (One-Page)

(Matches the version you approved)

Contract:

Focus for today: _____

Outcome by end: _____

Timebox: _____ minutes

Listen:

Current flow: _____

First friction point: _____

Last time it worked: _____

Explore (choose 1–2 levers):

☐ Clarity ☐ Rhythm ☐ Workflow ☐ Communication

☐ EnvironmentNotes: _____

Action (2-week pilot):

Change #1: _____ Owner: _____

Change #2: _____ Owner: _____

Success metric(s): _____

Check-ins: _____

Review:

What improved: _____

Keep / Modify / Retire: _____

B2. 3C Feedback Cue Card

Context: What outcome or expectation are we discussing?
Conduct: What specific behavior or pattern occurred?
Change: What does "next time" look like? What support is needed?

B3. 4R Weekly Coaching Cadence

1. **Recap:** What we agreed last week

2. **Results:** What worked, what didn't

3. **Refine:** One adjustment for the upcoming week

4. **Reset:** Confirm new commitments and dates

B4. Outcome Brief Template

Purpose: _____
  Definition of Done:
  -

  -

  -

  Success Criteria (quality/timing):

  Constraints:
  Owner: _____
  Milestones: _____

B5. RAID Ownership Matrix

Role	Person	Notes
R – Responsible		
A – Accountable		
I – Input		
D – Debrief		

B6. FAST Decision Framework

Frame: What decision must be made?
Assemble: Who provides input, and by when?
Set Criteria: What matters most—speed, cost, risk, impact?
Time: When the decision will be made and communicated?
  Decision Note Template:
- Decision + rationale

- Alternatives considered

- Risks + mitigations

- Next steps

- Owner

B7. Priority Board Guide

Use these labels:
- **HOT:** Immediate response required

- **PRIORITY SWAP:** A now outranks B

- **DELAY APPROVED:** New due date

- **HOLD:** Pause work

Team Priority Board fields:

B8. One-Page Accommodation Plan

Need Identified:

    Work Impact:

    Adjustment(s):

    Owner(s): _____
    Review Date: _____

Appendix C: Neuroinclusive Practices

These tools support team-level rituals, norms, and communication systems.

C1. Team Norms Starter Kit

Common neuroinclusive norms:
- We define outcomes before work begins.

- We label priority changes explicitly.

- We allow multiple modes of contribution.

- We document decisions within 24 hours.

- We respect deep-work blocks.

- We ask for clarity rather than assume intent.

C2. Meeting Modes Checklist

☐ Agenda shared 24 hours ahead
☐ Pre-reading available
☐ Clear meeting mode (Inform / Debate / Decide / Plan)
☐ Time-boxed sections

☐ Written follow-up within 24 hours
☐ Optional written participation
☐ Decision Note produced if needed

C3. Communication Systems Guidelines

Email: major updates, decisions, documentation
Chat: quick questions, light coordination
Docs: collaboration, drafts, shared writing
Meetings: clarification, discussion, relationship building
Teams choose and publish their communication rules.

C4. Culture Rituals Menu

Pick 1–2 rituals to strengthen inclusion:
- Weekly clarity reset

- Wins & Workflows review

- Decision Review Fridays

- Workstyle spotlights

- Monthly process tune-up

C5. Communication Alignment Checklist

Ensure your team's communication systems support clarity, predictability, and neuroinclusion.
A. Clarity of Intent

☐ Messages include purpose or context ("Why am I sharing this?").
☐ Action items are labeled clearly (e.g., **Action:** John — due Friday).
☐ Deadlines are explicit.
☐ "Definition of done" is included when assigning work.

☐ Priority changes are labeled (HOT, PRIORITY SWAP, HOLD, DELAY APPROVED).

B. Channel Discipline

☐ The team has agreed-upon rules for when to use:
- Chat

- Email

- Shared docs

- Meetings

☐ Decisions are always captured in writing.
☐ Drafts and collaboration happen in shared documents, not chat threads.
☐ Urgent communication has a standard protocol.

C. Processing-Friendly Communication

☐ Written follow-ups accompany verbal instructions.
☐ Important decisions are documented within 24 hours.
☐ Communication avoids vague phrasing or implied meaning.
☐ Employees have multiple ways to ask clarifying questions.
☐ Long or complex information is chunked into sections.

D. Predictability of Information Flow

☐ The team has predictable meeting cadences.
☐ Updates happen at known intervals (daily, weekly, etc.).
☐ Pre-reads are sent before meetings that require thoughtful input.
☐ Stakeholders receive decision notes on time.

E. Respect for Communication Preferences

☐ Team members share their preferred communication modes.
☐ The leader accommodates different processing speeds.
☐ Written feedback is available when verbal delivery may overwhelm.
☐ Camera-optional participation is normalized.
☐ Team norms support silence, reflection time, and asynchronous input.

F. Conflict & Clarification Protocol

☐ Team members use a "clarity-first" pass before escalating.
☐ Conflicts focus on content, not assumptions about intent.
☐ Ambiguity is resolved openly ("Here's what I understood…").
☐ Leaders model curiosity rather than defensiveness.

G. Inclusivity Signals

☐ Space is made for all communication styles.
☐ Employees are not penalized for needing clarity or repetition.
☐ Information is not hoarded or kept informal.
☐ Meetings allocate time for written or structured contributions.
☐ The team actively checks for misalignment.

Appendix D: Additional Resources

D1. Books & Articles

(List matches the References page you approved.)A curated list of foundational texts, leadership books, and neurodiversity research.

D2. Professional Associations

- SHRM

- HRCI

- ADA National Network

- Neurodiversity in Business Consortium

D3. Neurodiversity Training Resources

- MindEdge Neurodiversity Certificates

- Stanford Neurodiversity Project

- NeuroLeadership Institute

D4. Digital Tools for Focus & Organization

- Trello, Asana, ClickUp

- Notion

- Forest App

- Brain.fm

- Loop habit tracker

- Pomodoro timers

D5. Self-Assessments (with disclaimer)

(Not diagnostic; for insight only)
- ADHD screening questionnaires

- Autism spectrum self-reflection tools

- Sensory profile assessments

- Processing style questionnaires

Appendix E: Leadership Quick-Start Guide for Neuroinclusion

Purpose

A rapid-start tool for managers who want to support neurodivergent employees effectively.

Top Five Leadership Actions

1. **Be explicit, not implied** — ND employees thrive on clarity.

2. **Provide structure** — predictable routines reduce overwhelm.

3. **Coach through strengths** — performance improves more this way.

4. **Normalize processing time** — don't mistake pause for disengagement.

5. **Adjust environment** — small sensory changes go a long way.

Checklist: Am I Leading Inclusively?

- ☐ My instructions are clear, not abstract

- ☐ I give agendas before meetings

- ☐ I offer written expectations

- ☐ I recognize individual strengths

- ☐ I check in without micromanaging

- ☐ I avoid assuming "common sense"

- ☐ I follow predictable patterns when possible

Appendix F: Overwhelm Recovery & Regulation Plan

Purpose

To help ND employees anticipate and manage overwhelm before it becomes shutdown, burnout, or disengagement.

Step 1: Identify Your Overwhelm Signals

Check all that resonate:
- ☐ Difficulty initiating

- ☐ Task paralysis

- ☐ Emotional flooding

- ☐ Shutdown

- ☐ Irritability

- ☐ Avoidance

- ☐ Mental fog

- ☐ Sensory overload

Step 2: Build a Regulation Toolkit

Common examples:
- Sensory breaks

- Quiet workspace

- Breathing or grounding

- Movement

- Visual timers

- Clear prioritization

- Written task list

- Time blocking

- Short recovery pauses

Your toolkit:

Step 3: Create a Communication Plan (Optional)

If you need help from your supervisor:

"My workload is approaching overwhelm.To stay productive, I need to clarify priorities or adjust timelines.Can we review what's essential for today versus later in the week?"

Step 4: Overwhelm Action Plan

Trigger	Strategy	Support Needed (if any)

About the author

 **Jason Michaels, MBA, SPHR, SHRM-CP**, is a senior human resources professional with more than twelve years of experience supporting employees and leaders across complex organizational environments. His work spans employee relations, leadership development, organizational culture, DEI, performance management, operational planning, and workforce strategy.

Jason earned a Bachelor of Science in Organizational Psychology, grounding his career in the study of human behavior, motivation, cognitive functioning, and group dynamics in workplace settings. He later completed his Master of Business Administration, concentrating in Human Resources, Project Management, and Entrepreneurial Leadership—a combination that reflects his strength in both people systems and organizational structure.

He holds two of the HR industry's most respected professional credentials:

- **SPHR (Senior Professional in Human Resources)** — demonstrating advanced knowledge in strategic HR leadership, workforce planning, talent management, and organizational policy.

- **SHRM-CP (Society for Human Resource Management – Certified Professional)** — emphasizing applied HR expertise, behavior-based competency models, and practical decision-making.

Diagnosed with ADD at age five, Jason approaches workplace development with a blend of lived neurodivergent insight and extensive professional experience. Throughout his HR career, he has witnessed firsthand the challenges neurodivergent employees face in environments built for one standard of thinking—and he has coached leaders on how to build systems that help all employees perform at their highest level.

Jason is also the author of The Exit Interview for Stress, a book that explores burnout, emotional resilience, and sustainable work habits. Across all his writing and professional practice, his mission is consistent: help people understand how they work, not pressure them to work like everyone else.

Thrive & Lead reflects his commitment to building workplaces where cognitive diversity is recognized, respected, and transformed into meaningful performance and growth.

Learn more at **thejasonmichaels.com**.

www.ingramcontent.com/pod-product-compliance
Lightning Source LLC
Chambersburg PA
CBHW051630120626
46551CB00014B/2020